buttonmash

(buried under things that occupy naked minds and shameless hearts)

philip ofe

Copyright © 2019 Philip Ofe

All rights reserved.

ISBN: 9781077530126

DEDICATION

everyone mentioned in this book and you, the reader

CONTENTS

Acknowledgments	i
atcgb	1
icfgtsaipmo	3
mma4a pt.1	4
lhaloh, inej	5
ilayatom	7
gbimotl	9
mprisfu	10
ifahiton	11
mma4a pt.2 (b)	15
jatc	17
ttilaa	19
tiaagwiffbtshtf	21
tmib	23
tiadefm	24
mhasowgb	26
dpwme	27

abyss	28
phm	29
yattot	31
mma4a pt.3	32
apagbdiapagd	34
c/c	36
bb	39
ttiwtdy	41
mma4a pt.4	43
wywh	45
ty. iwittlm	46

ACKNOWLEDGMENTS

This project couldn't have happened without those who have supported me through many years of my life and have gone through to support me with my art too. I really appreciate all the help I've gotten with this book and I really hope you all enjoy your contributions.

Thank you

atcgb

we could sit around for hours,
watch the clouds go by.
we can talk and talk for ages until i
fall asleep in your lap, while you stroke my neck
as we watch the clouds go by.

and as the clouds go by, you
tell me what's on your mind
you wanna find the kind
of love that you see in the movies.
the kind of love that can't go to shit.
the kind of love where you're
    immersed in it.
as the clouds go by.

there was talk of the future, of us and the world.
    there was talk of our bodies, intertwined and curled.
we moved in our own unique and special way.
there was nothing that could ruin our day.
or so we thought
    as the clouds go by.

as the clouds go by, we argued for time.
you breathed, i sighed.
i raged, you cried.
we made up, raised up, fucked up and looked up
as the clouds go by.

    i would lay with you for hours on end.
    in you, i found not just a lover but a friend.
over time, things went bad and then you left.
for us, i thought it was the end. it was the end.
and i was still there, watching the clouds go by
without you

by my side.

icfgtsaipmo

my eyes just won't seem to close
i can't seem to sleep, not even a little doze
i'm wide awake at an ungodly hour in the morning, but it's not like i have nothing to do
i just don't want to do anything and that's cool.
i just want sleep, but sleep hasn't arrived yet
it's stuck in traffic or something, i bet

i'm wide awake and i'm not too happy about it
because now i have to use my mind and think or whatever seems fit
my mum used to say "close your eyes and think about sleep", that used to be the trick
but i think my head has gotten too slick, my brain isn't thick and knows what's up
i'd probably be better off connecting it to a brick... or a bat... or a blunt object, solid and quick
okay, i sound like a lunatic

but i'm wide awake, for god's sake
at an hour where in any moment, day will break
maybe that nap earlier was a total mistake...
with not much to do, i get up and i wander
with nothing to send me into slumber, i wonder
at what time will i fall asleep?
at what time will my mind no longer creep?
at what time...?

mma4a pt.1

what if i didn't eat that bagel on Tuesday?
what if we were cruising along the southern highway?
what if i couldn't see anymore?
what if i fell through the crust, disintegrating into the core?
what if i killed a being?
what if i wasn't just a fling?
what if the stars really told us who we are and we had our prophecies mapped out?
what if we really aren't alone in the universe and there are six more others like ours?
what if i could extend the hours?
what if i could produce flour?
what if, what if, what if?
what if we were married right now?
what if i was not allowed?
what if we should...
what if we were...
what if we could...

ihaloh, inej

to all the hoodies i've loved before,
you'll never be forgotten, that's for sure.
we'll start with honourable mentions
and then we'll crack down with my hoodie collection

there was the speckled grey zip up one, a young filly that kinda fit me silly (it was a fitted
medium and i had a bit of a belly).
you didn't last long but you were the gauze for my tattoo when i had to run for my coach
there's a metaphor for love somewhere in that line
there was an oversized grey one from my sister
she said to me she wouldn't miss it so i raised it as one of my own
until my friend took it and it was never seen again

to all the hoodies i love now,
there's 22 of you, oh wow
the twin leavers hoodies, burgundy and green
the olive/khaki one that's rarely ever been seen
the two reds: Maryland, the state and sadly not the cookies
the University of Kent one, have to represent, son!
the weird pastel blue one that says "staff"
the burgundy sidemen one, that's a laugh
the pink and the purple one, complete with matching bandanas
the yellow one that Donald Glover wore on his show, Atlanta
the zip up black and the zip up blue,
there's another black zip up that i own too
a grey one that says "one day more!"
the other grey one that's currently on the floor - welcome to Superbowl 48
guys, i'm a Seals fan now

there's a cobalt blue one that reminded me of a BROCKHAMPTON song
it's cool and little bit abstract like Kevin
don't know who Diana was but she was poppin' in '97

the "no problem" hoodie, shout out to chance the rapper
the Kent Snow one, don't ask me how i got it, i'm not even in the society
the school of arts one, of course in black
the other two performing arts hoodies, they go way back
there's the camel one that i got on sale that day
and finally, the one that makes me feel like Kanye

now i know you're thinking, "wow that's a lot"
yes, it is, and there's still more to cop
to all the hoodies i'll be with in the future,

wait for me my lovelies, i'm coming to get ya
and to all the hoodies here and now,
thank you for everything you represent but i won't go as far as to say you're heaven sent.

ilayatom

you ever just look at someone and you're like "oh my"?
you ever just look at someone and you think "be mine"?
let's just chill and talk for hours
for no occasion at all, let me bring you flowers
for no occasion at all, let's just sit in the shower
i think about you and me all the time
sitting in the sun, blowing dandelions for fun, in the bar, drinking a fuck ton
coming home to your warm embrace, kissing you everywhere on your face,
oh my

look at me when i look at you
i look so smitten and i know you think so too
look at me, damn...
i'm as short as Kendrick but my heart's got a big ass span, oh man....
it's obvious.
                              how can you be so oblivious?

i can never not notice you, you're like senpai
that's an anime joke, you'll get that in time, oh my.

my oh my, you make me sigh
my oh my, i figuratively want to die
i look at you and see what we could be
together, we could be amazing
we could be together? how amazing.
oh my, you make me swoon
you shine as brightly as the moon
to me, you're practically flawless
for you, i'm your addict, my heart is what you affect, sorry for being so direct
but oh my, you're perfect

gbimotl

your colours complement each other so nicely
i can't think where my gaze would rather be
the yellow
the green
the brown around the seams
your form knows no boundaries
you take any shape you want

that's what i love about you
that's why when i open my phone, you're the first thing i see
there are many words for how i feel about you
probably even more than twenty-two
just know that i cannot quit you
what you are doesn't need to be said, but for those wondering...

garlic bread.

mprisfu

my insanity grows like a tumour
disclaimer, this contains no humour
i guess i get my insanity from you
but you also gave me your patience too
i know it's not good to call you insane,
but you are for thinking that man will ever change.

he is who is.
you are who you are.
you're just as bad as him and to me, you've set the bar.
i can't say you're perfect but i love you as you are.
you've taught me many a thing and for that, i'm thanking God.

i'm thanking God for the both of you, for bringing me to life
but i question him as to why i live in your strife.
i'm thanking him for having a roof over my head
but i'm thinking why your arguments don't let me go to bed
i thank God for bringing you two together
but at times i wonder if you're weren't, would it be better?
would you both be happier if you went your separate ways?
i want to know what in the world compels you both to stay
you both say you love each other, but i know that's bullshit
if this is what your love is, then i want no part of it

ifahiton

since i could remember, i've always had an imaginary friend

someone i could talk to and play with for hours on end

i had siblings but they were older

the most i'd get is being put on their shoulders

i was in my own company a lot of the time and i guess it was fine because i always had a friend

in my head...

his name was Chris and i'd blame him for all the bad things i did

            who was i trying to kid?

i wasn't a good friend to a figment of my own imagination

i was unkind and mean towards my own creation

and as i grew, Chris faded away

i knew that he wouldn't be able to stay

he had to leave at some point and i had to be okay with that

i won't lie to you, there are days when he does come back

short and timely visits to check up on me and see if i'm okay

wouldn't be surprised if he came when i was old and grey.

i have a new imaginary friend and his name is Tim.

he isn't exactly imaginary as he's a plastic blow up alien

he has a vacant look and his green skin is so radiant

i talk to him every day and i must say, he's a really good listener.

i would say i substitute therapy for imaginary friends and plastic entities because i don't have the money or i choose not to talk to real people because i don't want to seem a certain type of way and say "i need help". i find it quite funny that to this day, i still have the need for a creation in my head to talk to in times of solitude. i wouldn't say i'm not all there but i wouldn't be surprised, nor would i care.

i wonder what Tim does when i leave the room

i wonder if he comes alive and starts to bloom

i wonder if he watches tv or reads a book

maybe he cuts the grass or tries to cook

if the toys from Toy Story can do it, why can't he?

i do sometimes wish he wasn't inanimate and that he would just be

but then a human friend would be what i need

and that's not the point of Tim

that's not the point of him.

he's there for me and me only

he's there for when i feel sad and lonely

and it's fitting he is what he is.

an alien.

something we have in common.

i sometimes feel alone and alienated in social groups and with people and topics of discussion.

to me, they feel like something out of this world.

i feel out of this world.

i sometimes wish i was out of this world.

like Tim.

like Chris.

a figment of one's imagination.

mma4a pt.2 (b)

breathe...
breathe...

i exhale in darkness
i inhale the harshness of the night.
my carcass breathes in the harsh pace that my brain seems to tarnish.
thinking is harmless.
it's the overthinking that prevents my catharsis.

breathe. sit in the dark of night and breathe.
there's nothing on my mind that seems to be
hypotheticals, theories and everything else that's dreary.
my thoughts are like a series
a series of the weird and the wonderful
a series of the uneasy and the comfortable.
(a series of staggered breaths)

my mind starts to drift at 26 minutes past 4...
i think of someone kicking down my door
i think of the tap that's drips drops more and more
i think of fornication and ejaculation
i think of a certain someone who fits that description
i think of where i will be in the span of 2/3 years, when i'm out of uni and pursuing my career
i think of her
i think of him
i think of how i'd rule if i was king
i think of mayo chickens and double cheeseburgers
i think of vines and memes and other random shit
i think of how the hell i got to this bit.
i think.

think.
thoughts and feelings skating round my mind like a rink

i sink...
not back into the softness of the bed but into my fucked-up head.
but then i remember...
to breathe.

jatc

i've spent a lot of my time looking for love, in places i saw fit
love in others, love in myself, love in that certain someone
but i never exactly found what i was looking for. i felt done.

the first place you'd seek or look for love is in your parents.
you try to see how they act with one another
you try and see if that's what you aim to be
that's something i never found in them.
failure at the first hurdle.

the second place is common and that's in others.
your friends, your sisters or your brothers
your first crush, your girlfriend or boyfriend
you wear your heart on your sleeve for it to break again and again
but it's practice, right?
you have to kiss a few frogs before you meet your prince type of shit
let me tell you, chief - that ain't it.

i want to tell you; you'll find love, because you will
but until that day, you've got a lot to get through
until that day, there will be times your heart will break in two
and until that day, you have to find love in you

the third place is hidden in plain sight
the nooks and crannies are gonna be tight
but you need to search the whole of your soul and find the love you need for yourself
be comfortable, be confident, be bae
if not today, then the next day or the day after that, maybe even on a Sunday
take your time to love yourself
you're not going anywhere
there's no rush to be your own crush

and once you fall in love with yourself,
you'll find the love you've seen everywhere else.
in the movies, in the books, in your parents, in your friends.
i'm in the process of loving myself and i could not be more excited to see what's to come
take your time, love yourself, then Cupid will find your sweet bum.

ttilaa

the crisp air as soon as you step outside
the small puddles drying up in the rising sun
the sound of the conkers as they collide
the perfect temperature that this season provides.

that's just the start.
the colours might be my favourite part
the orange, purple, the brown and yellow
just the feeling you get feels so mellow
the scent of the lady walking by with her pumpkin spiced everything
the way the robins get together to chirp and tweet and sing.

the harsh sunset gives us a beautiful end to the day
to pave way for the cold, long night
a night where you can still go on adventures and not get frostbite
then the soft sunrise commences and we get a glimpse of the purple twilight.

where the weather isn't too bad - perfect for a hoodie or a jacket.

when you can unapologetically wear plaid - clad head to toe, if you like.

when you can finally see your breath in the air, when you constantly experiment with footwear, when it's time to bring out the knitwear from the back of the closet somewhere, winter could never compare.

where the leaves fall every few seconds to float down to the ground, where you're surrounded by the vivid sounds of twigs snapping, birds singing, winds blowing, rain pattering, in the sun where the selfie lighting is quite flattering.

it doesn't allow for much to blossom,

but seriously, how awesome is autumn?

tiaagwiffbtshtf

i feel like shit.
i feel like a train's just hit.
fuck me, i'm in pain.
the same pain i've felt again and again, too many times to count now but the end result is always
the same.
i feel low and empty, worthless and lame.

i can't bear to close my eyes because you occupy my mind
i close my eyes and every time, it's you i find.
that's when i become sleepless,
that's when i become restless,
then i become reckless.

i tear the rest of myself apart.
i tear and tear until there's nothing but the shreds of my heart
i drink myself to the brink, i get so high, i can't come down, yet...
yet my brain doesn't seem to want to forget

forget our nights together
forget your scent
forget your eyes
forget your lips
forget your touch
forget your taste
forget you.
neither my heart, mind or soul wants to forget what we had, so what part of me does?

i can't forget our moments because then i'd be forgetting you and that's the last thing i want.
i can't forget you because you are the one thing i want.
if i were to forget you and everything we'd shared, i'd be back at square one.
wanting to burn up in the sun, wanting my life to just be done.

wanting to find peace of mind.

solitude.
i excel in solitude, yet i'm at my happiest when i'm with you.
you brought me from a dark place and now you've pushed me back in.
but i can't be that person that pulls you in too and so i have to forget you.

tmib

you pierce through the clouds, illuminating everything and anything you spot
you radiate in the darkness, guiding stragglers on their adventures
you influence the waters, gravitating back and forth to you
all while you sit there, wanting nothing more than to be seen, to be noticed,
aren't you keen?

eyes are in awe by you
subtle yet striking
cold but inviting
explored yet still a mystery
watching us through history

beautiful, you make me swoon
mesmerising, you are
the moon.

tiadefm

to me, it's a conundrum
i'll swipe left and right and then some
to what end? to what cost?
another connection's just been lost.
like that.

like that, they stop replying and you're left wondering where you fucked up
like that, you're left relying on hope and time and all that crap
just like that, it all comes to an end
then onto another newfound tinder friend.

am i doing this wrong? am i playing the cards right?
no-one's swept me off my feet, no "love" is in sight
like, i've had a couple encounters that have ended okay
but not in the way that i've wanted it, but hey - you win some, you lose some.

now i know what you're thinking:
dating apps are pointless and there's no use trying your luck
it's full of people just trying to find a quick fuck
you do find some gems who want more than sexual euphoria
though you'll cringe at some bios that get cornier and cornier.

i'm not saying i'm looking for the love of my life
but my experiences do always end in strife
deletion of it all will save me the hassle
the hassles of dating apps that leaves me baffled

mhasowgb

there are many forms you take, let's not forget
baguette
i can't discriminate because they're all so nice
a slice
you're beautiful, but if i carry on, you're going to make me fatter
ciabatta
sometimes i just can't get enough of you and it makes me lose my head
pizza bread
i never want to be without you, for you, i'd give my all
dough balls
i need you, you're my fix
bread sticks
just a bit of oil, sprinkle parsley on top, add some garlic to butter, as much as you want, don't stop
i don't care what you look like, you're tasty either way
garlic bread, you fucking beaut, you brighten up my day

dpwme

you take a look at me and what do you see?
a toy, a plaything, a phase or a fad.
you have your fun and throw me away when it gets bad.
false hope fills my brain and i get too complacent.
you bring me pain and you don't even fucking exchange it.
yet you replace it with apologetic words and sympathetic tones.
you run hurt through my fragile bones.

you seem empathetic. fuck you.
if you had any respect, you'd have stop yourself from inflicting the same pain you've once felt before.
but instead you knew what it was that you tore.

don't play with me if you can't afford to fix me when i break,
because how would you feel if your heart was at stake?

abyss

it's easier to sink than to stay afloat
when you're on the brink of collapse in an empty sea
my oar has snapped, there's a small hole in the bottom of the boat and i'm
running out of time

land is nowhere to be found
i can't hear the doves make a sound
i can't see anything but the sea
i can't see anything but me

in the abyss.

cold and dark, unnerving but no shark.
at least not yet.
the hole will soon fill up and i'll join whatever is down there.

phm

you ever felt like you were trapped?
like you're stuck in a box, six feet underground with no way out?
you could scream and shout, but no one would hear your cries.
you tell everyone you're good but you know it's just lies.
they know it's just lies.
your face is a lie, the way you move is a lie, the words you speak are just lies.
your dead eyes show the lies about how you really feel on the inside...
trapped and alone and nowhere feels like home.

you're past the point of breaking and in your own mind you're forsaking yourself.
you tell yourself you don't mean anything and that you wouldn't be missed if you happened to go.
you don't feel wanted and you never have.
it's all a facade to help the days go by just that little bit easier.
why do you feel like this?
why do i feel like this?

do i strive for unhappiness
at any cost?

i guess sadness is all i've ever know
it's hard
for old habits to
get lost

i am lost. tell me the way home.
tell me how to rid myself of these feelings.
i can do it; i promise i can do it.

yattot

you at the table over there
you with the tall cup of coffee
you with the dirty blonde hair
you with the dark grey and slightly stained hoodie

you with your red spotted cheeks
you, who only ever orders the same drink always
you, the one who laughs but doesn't speak
you, who gets frustrated at your laptop and taps furiously when it starts slowing down
you, reading that one famous book by John Green

you with the cute smile
you with the perfect eyes
literally, like just the right size
i just wanted to say, hey.

mma4a pt.3

a stream of consciousness, that's all this is...

stranger things
danger brings
fear
fear in losing myself, in losing those around me, in losing my head
i see you, stop dead
dead in my tracks
i look at you and fall all over again
and we're falling, and we're falling and we stop
and we're falling, and we're falling, too far now from the drop
a little bit of air resistance would be nice
a little bit longer and my heart will splice

running
to where? who knows?
to whom? who cares?
just run
we're running from the past because we hate to reflect
put on the masquerade mask and join the party
learn the etiquette, let it not be a farce
put on the mask and hide your true self
build that wall
you've given your all
way. too. many. times.

limes
break out the tequila and drown your sorrows
get fucking wasted and go again tomorrow
don't let it catch up to you, just keep on going
what else would you rather be doing?
who else would you rather be doing?
you feel empty, don't you?
fill yourself up

however you want to
just fill yourself up
not with the bad stuff, just the good stuff
okay, maybe a bit of the bad stuff, it'll make you resilient, make you tough
order and chaos are meant to be
give it a little longer, trust me
you'll see.

apagbdiapagd

you know, i get really jealous of lightweights
they don't spend as much time and money getting drunk
a couple drinks in and they're already crunk
i wish i was a lightweight, how great would that be
for me, that'd be amazing, because i love drunk me

drunk me doesn't like to make trouble
drunk me just pours out the doubles
drunk me is loud and that is a good thing
although, drunk me will drink whatever you bring
drunk me loves a drink in his hand at all times
drunk me will probably do a tequila with the lime

after a night out, where do you go?
the kebab shop, McDonald's?
drunk me would go home
not because i wouldn't want to carry on the night, oh no
because sober me is clever and bright
sober me looks out for drunk me, that's facts
sober me would've left garlic bread in the freezer at the back

drunk me would easily make the garlic bread for takeaway
because drunk me would want to party till the break of day
singing aye, let's get it, let's drink some more
as long as there's garlic bread, i'm a garlic bread whore
pour another one, don't be a bore
the sesh is life, it isn't a chore
i implore you to carry on with much vigour
drink until the sun comes up, then get ready for the encore

c/c

i'd be lying if i said i was torn
i'd be lying if i said i couldn't choose between my two homes
i know exactly where i'd go
there's no place like home
there's no place other than home, where i feel like breaking

a place that's meant to be my safety, my shelter
if i had the option, my exit would be helter-skelter
if i could, i'd leave in a heartbeat
off we go, off on my feet, no looking back, no slowing down, not even a frown
just off out of town.

strange, how i enjoy my life eighty-nine miles away
my life that constantly tests my mental state practically everyday
but i find a way and weigh up my options, i play the cards and embrace the situation because come what may, that's all i can say to stay up because there's no way i'll let myself fall back down to that place.
not only is it not safe in original home, but it ain't safe up in my head
and so that's why instead, you'd sooner find me eighty-nine miles away from this place i call home.

the city vs the country - both full of pros and cons
they both offer me some kind of solace
the city has such life and is full of opportunity
the country has the peace and quiet, that i so often dream of
the city is bustling
the country is humbling
the country is so chill
the city has its thrills, with its concrete hills and overlapping sound spills, your mind is always full, no need for a refill

however, the city can be cruel
too much opportunity to create a naive fool

noise stretching miles and miles
a bright, light polluted sky forces you to look at the map on your phone
rather than the map up above, a map cemented for centuries
a place where your fear is sensory and significant in making enemies, the city.

the country can be haunting
sometimes no light for miles makes walking at night quite daunting
the constant walking leaves you tired and restless forcing you to become breathless
but the number of cafes is endless, so that's a plus, i guess?
less people around means one can be reckless and left feeling relentless
and at night, anxious.
nightfall in the country is scarily mesmerising
the silence among the starry sky is compromising and surprising, yet tranquilising and tantalising

as tranquil and haunting it may seem,
i believe right now, the country is for me
my mind at ease
in the city, my mind is harder to appease
where i'll end up, i have no guarantees.

bb

coconut. Oreo. Bounty. these are some of the names that spring into my mind that people have called me and i just don't get it. i just don't get it.

what does it mean to be black?
does it mean playing the race card and asking for some slack?
does it mean being obliged to love hip hop?
do i have to wear my jeans to my knees till i drop?
do i have to chat like i'm from ends, fam?
or do i have talk like my brothers from the land of Uncle Sam?

i talk white? are you saying that out of spite because i'm well spoken? but you'd rather see me act token?
lift me up, brother, don't put me down
there are more pressing issues for us, but you'd rather me drown.
drown in insecurity for who i am.
i'm sorry, but that just can't stand.

according to particular groups in society, i'm a "white person".
because of my hobbies, my interests and sometimes even what i wear.
you're a coconut, you're such a Bounty,
that's all i ever hear.
"you're not black, if you like this, you can't class yourself as a black person."
really?

if i can't be my own person, then what's the point of being alive?
i'm not living to be defined as white or black
and i'm sure as hell not asking for you to cut me some slack, black.

we're all in the same boat facing the same struggles, yet you decide to belittle your fellow man because he doesn't act like you do. you fool.

infighting for what? what spot? what are you going to gain from it? throwing your fellow man into a pit? i am who i am and that is a black man.

what does it mean to be black?

it doesn't matter. by the colour of my skin, i define as black. if that's not enough for you lot, then i don't know. i shouldn't have to feel so attacked. i am black and that's a fact.

ttiwdty

your hands trail along my skin, goose bumps rise but i keep my eyes on the prize.
my lips part as i quiver at your touch and i let out exasperated gasps and on your thigh, my hand clasps.

i lower my head, gazing intently, intensely, consequently.
my fingers slither down your body, searching for their point of entry.
i start to caress gently.

"my god, the things i would do to you..."

my thoughts start to run wild, bursting to form into reality.
your moans are freed from your mouth, then you softly call out to me.
placing kisses on your neck, i kiss a trail down to your centre.
my eyes look up to yours, asking "please, may i enter?"

as you drip, my tongue takes a taste, not letting any of it go to waste.
your moans grow louder as my tongue goes to work, getting you to a point where your body starts to jerk. i smirk.

i crawl back up, to gaze into your eyes.
a sudden gasp as i push myself inside.
your eyes roll back as your centre divides.
soft and gentle, as our pelvises collide.

soft grunts escape my mouth as your nails dig in deeper.
audible moans are heard as i go in deeper.
you call out my name which makes me more eager.

you hold my stomach and i hold your legs.
we catch each other's gaze, it's your eyes that beg.
beg me to stop because it's too much.
beg me to carry on with my sensual touch.
beg me because it hurts so good.

beg me because you feel like you should.

beg for me, my love.
beg to let me do the things i'm thinking of.

mma4a pt.4

is my mind empty for the first time?
have i finally run out of bullshit to say?
do you think it'll last?
do you think they'll finally stop talking? Tim and Chris, that is.

silence is truly deafening
for my mind, my health
i should be
           bettering.

this won't be the last time i'll be awake at this hour
at this hour where my thoughts usually turn sour
if i had the power, i'd think of gumdrops and roses
but even my head knows the threat a rose poses.

i want to see you
                            bloom
i want you naked in my

you still inject hurt through my
                            veins
you still run cross country right around in my

i want a milkshake
i want to go to Japan
i want to take from you whatever i can
i want to be free
i want to fucking scream and shout
let's go to the sea and maybe just fuck about

this is a stream
and my head is the highest point
watch my thoughts trickle out
as i roll this joint

let's lift our heads up, all while getting closer and closer
in the dark, where my hands run you over and over
map out the stars with me
let's find a planetary body
so i can eventually push you away to go and inhabit that planet so you won't
ever have to see my face again

Tim, take me with you when you leave the earth
i want to venture the stars, give my mind a rebirth

give my heart

                                        a rebirth

give myself

                                        a rebirth

just so i cannot
hurt.

wywh

thoughts of you enter my mind but they are fleeting
only to return when my eyelids are shut and i am sleeping
a lot can happen in a dream that one cannot remember
however, you seem to be a constant member

i look around this room and see nothing but you
you sat on the desk chair, writing a song
you looking out the window, watching birds flying along
cross legged on the bed, rolling a joint for us to share
laying in the sheets, playing with a tiny tear

although thoughts of you are fleeting, you always seem to make your way back
in ways that are delightful and strange, in fact
scenario after scenario, you're always in my head
from the beginning at a, all the way to z

i sometimes wish i didn't think of you so
only because these thoughts can go
come today, gone tomorrow, in times of happiness and of sorrow
i wish you were here, live in the flesh
your presence and scent, live and fresh
i wish you were here, here by my side
and not only where my thoughts reside.

ty, iwttlm

as most people do, i struggle with loving myself
i struggle with finding my worth and acknowledging who i am to those around me
instead i tend to focus on the flaws inside and out me
instead i let the insecurities use my body, conveying a me that shouldn't be
this is a common thing
and i know i'm not alone in this

we need support, a helping hand
and that comes in the form of those who genuinely want to see us proudly stand and say "i love who i am".
i truly cannot say i'm there but i have those hands and i love them
so i wanted to say thank you for being you

thank you for picking up the phone in the middle of the night
thank you for calling me out on my spite
thank you for making me smile
thank you for going the extra mile, just to make me happy
thank you for being there through many episodes
thank you for making laugh when i feel crappy
thank you for helping me out through tough times
thank you for all your shoulders absorbing my tears
thank you for listening to me rant and not bleeding from your ears
thank you for the years you've spent by my side
thank you for calming down the tide
thank you for raising me up when i feel down
thank you so much for not letting me drown
thank you for that twenty you sent me when i couldn't ask for it anywhere else
thank you for helping me find a vice
thank you for telling me when i'm not being nice
thank you for all the solid advice, even the shitty stuff too
thank you for being you
thank you for the love

thank you for the hate
thanks for sticking it out when i get irate
thank you for letting me stay over
thank you for getting closer, not letting me be a loner

i promise i will keep on finding that self-love you talked of

if you're reading this and feel lonely in this world, know that there are really people around you that love and care for you so much

in fact, tell them:
    thank you for letting me know it's okay to be heartfelt, that it's okay for someone to really be themselves

        thank you, i will try to love myself.

as the clouds go by
i can't fucking get to sleep and it's pissing me off
my mind at 4am part 1
i have a lot of hoodies, i'm not even joking
i look at you and think oh my
garlic bread is the love of my life
my parent's relationship is so fucked up
imaginary friends are helpful in times of need
my mind at 4am part 2 (breathe)
just around the corner
the things i love about autumn
this is about a girl who i felt for but then shit hit the fan
the moon is beautiful
tinder is a dead end for me
might have a slight obsession with garlic bread
don't play with my emotions
a boy yearns soul saving
please help me
you at the table over there
my mind at 4am part 3
a poem about garlic bread disguised in a poem about getting drunk
country/city
being black
the things i would do to you
my mind at 4am part 4
wish you were here
thank you, i will try to love myself

Printed in Great
Britain
by Amazon